Our Changing Planet

Contents

Features

FAST FACTS

How long would it take to tunnel through Earth? Turn to page 5 to find out.

Do you know that in 1910 a scientist noticed Earth's land areas look like a giant jigsaw puzzle? Read about his discovery on page 7.

PROFILE

WORD BUILDER

What sort of waves are under Earth's surface? Find out on page 9.

Do you eat food that is grown in a maze? Find out more in **Battling Erosion** on page 20.

IN THE NEWS

SITESEEING · WATER, EARTH, & SKY

How long does a volcanic eruption last?

Visit **www.rigbyinfoquest.com**
for more about **VOLCANOES.**

What Is Earth?

Our planet, Earth, is one of many large rocks that travel around the sun. Nine planets and many moons all share our part of the universe. One moon travels around Earth, but some planets have no moon at all, and some have more than one. Together, the planets and moons form the solar system.

Earth's address in the solar system is Number 3, or third rock from the sun!

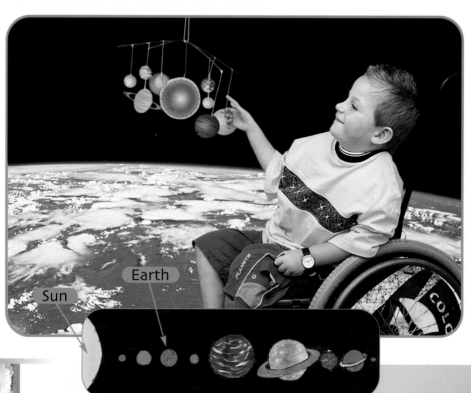

Earth

Sun

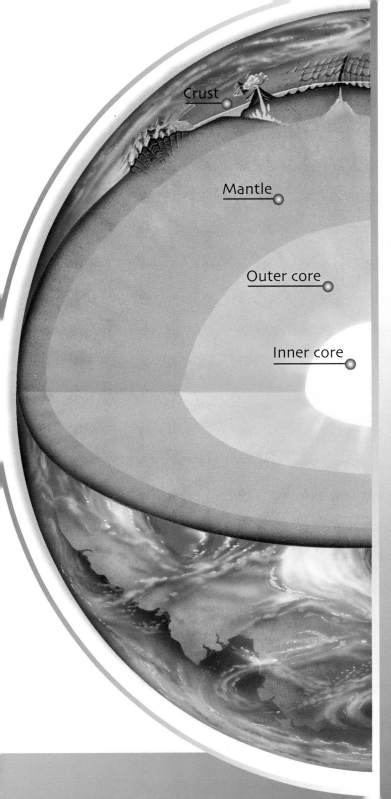

Crust

Mantle

Outer core

Inner core

Earth is made up of several layers. The surface is called the *crust*. There are two layers of rock beneath the crust that form the *mantle.* Beneath the mantle is the *outer core*, made mainly of boiling liquid iron. The *inner core* is the center of Earth. It is made of solid iron and nickel.

Scientists have figured that it would take 87 years to tunnel through Earth!

Our Restless Earth

Earth's crust is like a huge jigsaw puzzle made up of large and small pieces called **plates.** There are ocean plates and land plates. Hot, liquid rock called **magma** lies beneath the plates. The magma moves between the plates and pushes them around. The plates cannot go far before they collide with each other.

These pictures show how Earth's **continents** have moved over millions of years. They are still moving today.

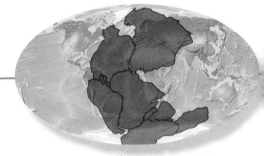

200 million years ago

Cross Section of Plate Movement

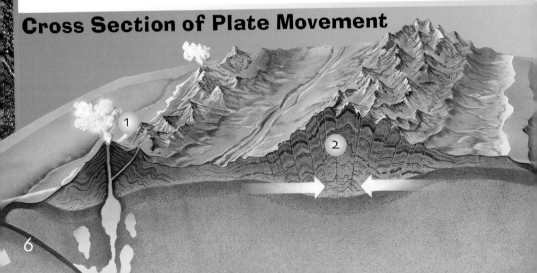

Alfred Wegener (1880–1930) was a German scientist. In 1910, he noticed that the continents look like puzzle pieces. His theory was that they once formed a single continent, which he called Pangaea. In the 1960s, after more studies, scientists finally accepted this theory.

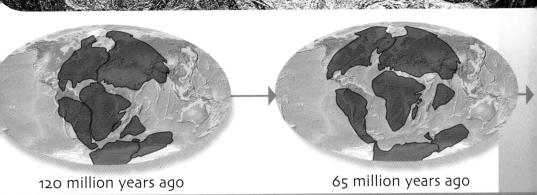

120 million years ago   65 million years ago

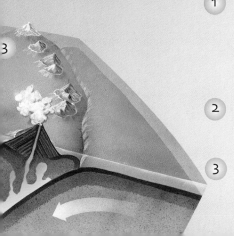

1. When an ocean plate meets a continental plate, the thin ocean plate is pulled down and volcanoes are formed.

2. When two continental plates crash, mountains are formed.

3. When two ocean plates meet, a string of islands is formed.

7

Shake and Shatter

Every 30 seconds, Earth shakes slightly. Most of these **tremors** are too small to be felt, but they are recorded by special instruments.

Earthquakes happen when plates collide and cause Earth's crust to break open. The break sends shock waves shooting through the surrounding rocks. This causes the ground on the surface to shake. If the earthquake is strong, it may topple buildings, collapse bridges and roads, and change the shape of the land.

Waves from underground collisions are called *seismic waves.* People who study these are called *seismologists.* These words come from the Greek word *seismos,* which means "earthquake."

Nearly 1,900 years ago, a Chinese man named Zhang Heng made an instrument that detected earthquakes. If the ground shook, a bronze ball fell from each dragon's mouth into the mouth of a frog below.

9

Rivers of Fire

Deep inside Earth, magma moves upward, trying to find a way to the surface. As Earth's plates move, cracks can let the magma through to explode as a volcano.

Some volcanoes are active, erupting at any time. Some are dormant, waiting to erupt. Others are extinct, or dead. Volcanoes have shaped many of Earth's islands, mountains, and plains. They have caused changes in the weather. They have buried cities and destroyed plant and animal life.

SITESEEING • WATER, EARTH, & SKY •

How long does a volcanic eruption last? Visit **www.rigbyinfoquest.com** for more about **VOLCANOES.**

Volcanologists are scientists who study volcanoes. They use instruments to help predict when eruptions may occur. Sometimes robot volcanologists are used to explore inside volcano craters. Dante II, shown below, is a robot volcanologist.

Dante II was sent inside the active crater of Mount Spurr in Alaska, United States.

Krakatau Blows!

In August 1883, a large volcanic eruption blew apart the island of Krakatau in Indonesia. The boom from the explosion was one of the loudest ever recorded. It was heard over 2,000 miles away. Clouds of ash and dust rose high into the air and circled Earth. When the volcano fell in on itself, giant waves called **tsunamis** were started.

Effects Around the World

1. The night sky over London, England was filled with beautiful colors.

2. Giant waves destroyed riverboats in Calcutta, India.

3. In Trinidad, the sun looked blue.

4. The eruption was heard as far away as Madagascar.

5. There was a tsunami in Perth, Australia.

Most of the island was destroyed when the volcano erupted.

Krakatau, Indonesia

2

5

Wear and Tear

Earth cannot protect itself from **weathering.**
Weather conditions such as snow, ice, heat,
wind, and rain split and crumble Earth's rocks.
Parts of Earth's surface are always being
soaked, dried out, frozen, or burned. Over time,
rocks are worn away, and the surface changes
shape. Rivers, oceans, and **glaciers** also grind
away at Earth's surface. This process is
called **erosion.**

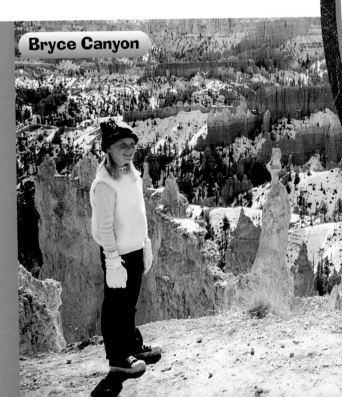

Bryce Canyon

At Bryce Canyon
in the United States,
weathering and
erosion have shaped
the stone into tall
columns called
hoodoos.

Glaciers move slowly downhill.
They grind away the rock,
forming U-shaped valleys.

15

Coastal Erosion

The ocean coasts are always changing shape. Wind and waves beat against cliffs. This breaks down rocks and shifts sand, forming beaches and sand dunes.

In some areas where a river enters a sea, soil and rocks, that the water carried away from riverbanks, are dropped. At these river mouths, called deltas, the soil and rocks build up over time, making smaller streams of water and more dry land.

The Mississippi River in the United States forms a delta where it enters the Gulf of Mexico.

The Changing Coastline

1. Waves eat away at the cliffs.
2. Sea stacks remain when the rock has been eaten away.
3. Blowholes form when the sea tunnels through the land.
4. Waves make rocky terraces at the cliff base.
5. Rocks from far inland may be found at the river mouth.
6. Sand dunes form when sand is blown into small hills.

17

The Human Factor

Our planet cannot protect itself from people. People build cities, roads, and bridges. They dam rivers for drinking water and electricity. They tunnel through mountains and dig deep for Earth's gems, minerals, and gas. They cut down forests for timber and clear land for houses and farms.

Earth has many useful resources. People are learning to carefully plan the changes they make to Earth's surface so they can help protect these resources.

People tunnel through Earth looking for resources.

Many countries need dams to make electricity. However, building a dam disturbs a river and the land around it. It is important to plan a dam carefully so there is little damage to the land, its plants, and the animals that live there.

Battling Erosion

Some creative farmers have come up with special ways to stop erosion of their farmland. They plant more than one crop at a time, and they plant their crops in strips that follow the shape of the land. They also make special waterways to carry water down slopes.

This sort of planting can prevent three-fourths of farmland erosion. It also makes some unusual crop patterns!

This pattern controls soil erosion on a small hill that slopes down from the center. The green crop is pasture grasses. The bare strips will be planted with corn.

A giant maze of corn and alfalfa keeps the soil in place. Erosion is cut down, and the soil is protected so that it can be used again.

Glossary

continent – one of the seven main land areas of Earth's surface

erosion – the action of wearing away slowly, especially by water, wind, or ice

glacier – a large amount of ice and snow that moves very slowly down a mountain

magma – hot liquid rock beneath the surface of Earth. When magma escapes through a volcano, it is called lava.

plate – a large moving area of land or ocean floor. Earth is made up of several main plates.

tremor – a movement of Earth's crust. Special equipment is needed to detect small tremors.

tsunami – (*soo NAH mee*) a huge, powerful wave that reaches up from an ocean's floor to its surface. A tsunami builds up as it races across the ocean and crashes onto the land.

volcanologist – a scientist who studies volcanoes

weathering – the breaking up or fading action upon a natural material that is done by water, air, the sun, and the freezing and melting of ice

Index

orth America

—— South America

┌— Europe

┌— Asia

Australia

└— Africa

—— Antarctica

Discussion Starters

1 Earthquakes can happen when people least expect them. How could you keep safe if an earthquake began to rumble while you were at school? What would you do if you were at home?

2 Over time, people have made many changes to Earth's surface, especially in cities. As our cities grow, we need to make more changes such as making new buildings and roads. What might be some of the careful planning that has to go into any changes we make in our cities? Why?

3 Earth is the third rock from the sun. It has just the right temperature for life. It's not too hot or too cold. What else does our planet have that makes it a good home?